Simple and Delicious Pinwheels

Easy Appetizer, Snack, and A Quick Lunch

BY: TRISTAN SANDLER

)◉◉◉◉◉◉◉◉◉◉◉◉◉◉◉◉◉◉◉◉(

License Notes

Let's get right into it because I wouldn't say I like fluff (you will see this in my recipes):

You aren't allowed to make any print or electronic reproductions, sell, re-publish, or distribute this book in parts or as a whole unless you have express written consent from me or my team.

Why? I worked really hard to put this book together and, if you share it with others through those means, I will not get any recognition or compensation for my effort. Not only that, but it's impossible to know how my work will be used or for what purposes. Thus, please refrain from sharing my work with others. Oh, and be careful when you're in the kitchen! My team and I aren't liable for any damages or accidents that occur from the interpretations of our recipes. Just take it easy and stay safe in the kitchen!

◖◉◉◉◉◉◉◉◉◉◉◉◉◉◉◉◉◉◉◉◉◉◉◗

Table of Contents

Introduction

Pinwheels are a simple appetizer or a light lunch. Preparing won't take much of your precious time, and you already have the ingredients in your pantry. The secret to preparing the most delicious pinwheels is to prepare a filling rich with flavors. The cream cheese enhanced with different spices and ingredients will create a delicious meal for you and your family.

Whether you prefer bacon and jalapeno, turkey and cheddar, or pesto and sundried tomatoes, you will always find the right fit for your taste. The best thing is that you can double the batch and prepare them ahead. Keep in mind that the pinwheels will do fine in the fridge for 3 to 4 days. But you can also freeze them for up to 2 months and always have a tasty appetizer ready for your guests.

Are you ready to discover the fantastic flavors? Let's get into this culinary journey together and pick the right fit for your taste!

1. Bacon jalapeno pinwheels

When you love spicy food, the bacon jalapeno pinwheels will amaze you. With the perfect amount of spiciness and creaminess, they will become your favorite appetizer. You can choose any hard cheese to your likings, such as cheddar or parmesan.

Time: 2 hours 15 minutes

Servings: 24 pinwheels

Ingredients

- 3 large flour tortillas

Filling

- 8 oz package of cream cheese
- 1 cup shredded hard cheese
- ½ cup cooked and crumbled bacon
- 1 jalapeno pepper, finely chopped
- ½ teaspoon garlic powder
- ½ teaspoon smoked paprika
- ¼ teaspoon salt

Instructions

Add the pinwheel filling ingredients into a large bowl. Mix well until incorporated. The cream cheese should be softened at room temperature to be easy to work with.

Lay your tortillas on the working surface and divide the filling mixture among them. Make sure to spread it evenly.

Roll each tortilla tightly and wrap it with plastic wrap.

Let the filled tortillas chill in the fridge for at least 2 hours to make slicing easier.

When the tortillas are chilled, remove the wrap and slice them into 1-inch pieces. Serve and enjoy.

2. Turkey pinwheels

If you have turkey slices handy, this recipe is the one for you. The combination of cream cheese and ranch dressing will add flavor to this recipe. Feel free to double the batch and welcome your guests with joy.

Time: 2 hours 15 minutes

Servings: 24 pinwheels

Ingredients

- 3 large flour tortillas
- ½ pound turkey slices

Filling

- 8 oz cream cheese
- ½ cup cooked and crumbled bacon
- 1 tablespoon ranch dressing
- 1 cup shredded cheddar cheese
- ¼ teaspoon salt

Instructions

Add the pinwheel filling ingredients into a large bowl. Mix well until incorporated. The cream cheese should be softened at room temperature to be easy to work with.

Lay your tortillas on the working surface and divide the filling mixture among them. Make sure to spread it evenly. Add three turkey slices for each.

Roll each tortilla tightly and wrap it with plastic wrap.

Let the filled tortillas chill in the fridge for at least 2 hours to make slicing easier.

When the tortillas are chilled, remove the wrap and slice them into 1-inch pieces. Serve and enjoy.

3. Red pepper pinwheels

The intense flavor of red peppers dominates in this recipe. Complemented with cheddar cheese, it is the ultimate gourmet pleasure for a Friday movie night. If you prefer spicy, you can add red pepper flakes.

Time: 2 hours 15 minutes

Servings: 24 pinwheels

Ingredients

- 3 large flour tortillas

Filling

- 8 oz package of cream cheese
- 1 cup shredded cheddar cheese
- ½ cup chopped roasted red peppers
- ¼ teaspoon salt
- 1 teaspoon onion powder

Instructions

Add the pinwheel filling ingredients into a large bowl. Mix well until incorporated. The cream cheese should be softened at room temperature to be easy to work with.

Lay your tortillas on the working surface and divide the filling mixture among them. Make sure to spread it evenly.

Roll each tortilla tightly and wrap it with plastic wrap.

Let the filled tortillas chill in the fridge for at least 2 hours to make slicing easier.

When the tortillas are chilled, remove the wrap and slice them into 1-inch pieces. Serve and enjoy.

4. Mexican pinwheels

Mixing pepper jack cheese, corn, and taco seasoning will recreate your favorite Mexican meal. Serve this as complementary to a meal or tasty finger food for game night.

Time: 2 hours 15 minutes

Servings: 24 pinwheels

Ingredients

- 3 large flour tortillas

Filling

- 8 oz package of cream cheese
- 1/2 cup shredded pepper jack cheese
- 1 cup shredded cooked chicken
- 1/4 cup corn canned
- ¼ cup green onions chopped
- ¼ teaspoon salt
- ½ teaspoon onion powder
- ½ teaspoon taco seasoning

Instructions

Add the pinwheel filling ingredients into a large bowl. Mix well until incorporated. The cream cheese should be softened at room temperature to be easy to work with.

Lay your tortillas on the working surface and divide the filling mixture among them. Make sure to spread it evenly.

Roll each tortilla tightly and wrap it with plastic wrap.

Let the filled tortillas chill in the fridge for at least 2 hours to make slicing easier.

When the tortillas are chilled, remove the wrap and slice them into 1-inch pieces. Serve and enjoy.

5. Buffalo chicken pinwheels

If you are one of the people that loves buffalo chicken, this recipe will exceed your expectations. The spicy filling will amaze you, so be sure to prepare a double batch for the whole week.

Time: 2 hours 15 minutes

Servings: 24 pinwheels

Ingredients

- 3 large flour tortillas

Filling

- 8 oz package of cream cheese
- 5 oz hot sauce
- 2 cups shredded and cooked chicken
- 1 cup shredded hard cheese
- ½ cup
- ¼ teaspoon salt
- ½ teaspoon garlic powder

Instructions

Add the pinwheel filling ingredients into a large bowl. Mix well until incorporated. The cream cheese should be softened at room temperature to be easy to work with.

Lay your tortillas on the working surface and divide the filling mixture among them. Make sure to spread it evenly.

Roll each tortilla tightly and wrap it with plastic wrap.

Let the filled tortillas chill in the fridge for at least 2 hours to make slicing easier.

When the tortillas are chilled, remove the wrap and slice them into 1-inch pieces. Serve and enjoy.

6. Italian pinwheels

The combination of pepperoni, hard salami, and provolone cheese will add tons of flavor. In addition, layering them will create an excellent presentation. The grated parmesan in the filing will also add flavor, making a versatile appetizer to go with a glass of Aperol spritz.

Time: 2 hours 15 minutes

Servings: 24 pinwheels

Ingredients

- 3 large flour tortillas
- 9 slices provolone cheese
- 9 slices of hard salami
- 9 slices pepperoni

Filling

- 8 oz package of cream cheese
- 1 cup pepperoncini
- 1/4 cup grated parmesan
- ¼ teaspoon salt

Instructions

Add the pinwheel filling ingredients into a large bowl. Mix well until incorporated. The cream cheese should be softened at room temperature to be easy to work with.

Lay your tortillas on the working surface and lay the pepperoni, hard salami, and provolone cheese. Divide the filling mixture among them and make sure to spread it evenly.

Roll each tortilla tightly and wrap it with plastic wrap.

Let the filled tortillas chill in the fridge for at least 2 hours to make slicing easier.

When the tortillas are chilled, remove the wrap and slice them into 1-inch pieces. Serve and enjoy.

7. Pickle pinwheels

This recipe shows you how to make delicious pinwheels with only a few ingredients. The combination of hard cheese, cream cheese, pickles, and ham is simple yet astonishing.

Time: 2 hours 15 minutes

Servings: 24 pinwheels

Ingredients

- 3 large flour tortillas

Filling

- 8 oz package of cream cheese
- 1/2 cup shredded Colby jack cheese
- ½ cup finely chopped dill pickles
- ½ cup chopped deli ham
- ¼ teaspoon salt

Instructions

Add the pinwheel filling ingredients into a large bowl. Mix well until incorporated. The cream cheese should be softened at room temperature to be easy to work with.

Lay your tortillas on the working surface and divide the filling mixture among them. Make sure to spread it evenly.

Roll each tortilla tightly and wrap it with plastic wrap.

Let the filled tortillas chill in the fridge for at least 2 hours to make slicing easier.

When the tortillas are chilled, remove the wrap and slice them into 1-inch pieces. Serve and enjoy.

8. Chicken bacon pinwheels

The rich bacon flavor paired with juicy chicken makes this recipe special. You can replace the cheddar cheese with any other hard cheese that suits your taste.

Time: 2 hours 15 minutes

Servings: 24 pinwheels

Ingredients

- 3 large flour tortillas

Filling

- 8 oz package of cream cheese
- 1 cup shredded cheddar cheese
- 1 cup cooked and shredded chicken
- ½ cup cooked and chopped bacon
- 1 tablespoon ranch dressing
- ¼ teaspoon salt
- ½ teaspoon garlic powder

Instructions

Add the pinwheel filling ingredients into a large bowl. Mix well until incorporated. The cream cheese should be softened at room temperature to be easy to work with.

Lay your tortillas on the working surface and divide the filling mixture among them. Make sure to spread it evenly.

Roll each tortilla tightly and wrap it with plastic wrap.

Let the filled tortillas chill in the fridge for at least 2 hours to make slicing easier.

When the tortillas are chilled, remove the wrap and slice them into 1-inch pieces. Serve and enjoy.

9. Mediterranean pinwheels

The combination of Mediterranean flavors is the secret to his delicious recipe. The feta adds a rich flavor, while the sun-dried tomatoes enhance the pinwheels with their aroma.

Time: 2 hours 15 minutes

Servings: 24 pinwheels

Ingredients

- 3 large flour tortillas

Filling

- 8 oz package of cream cheese
- ½ cup crumbled feta
- 1/4 cup sundried tomatoes
- ¼ teaspoon salt
- 1 teaspoon dried basil

Instructions

Add the pinwheel filling ingredients into a large bowl. Mix well until incorporated. The cream cheese should be softened at room temperature to be easy to work with.

Lay your tortillas on the working surface and divide the filling mixture among them. Make sure to spread it evenly.

Roll each tortilla tightly and wrap it with plastic wrap.

Let the filled tortillas chill in the fridge for at least 2 hours to make slicing easier.

When the tortillas are chilled, remove the wrap and slice them into 1-inch pieces. Serve and enjoy.

10. Chicken parmesan pinwheels

If you have leftover chicken from last night's dinner or bought rotisserie chicken, check out this recipe. The parmesan cheese, garlic powder, and chicken create a fantastic combination of flavors.

Time: 2 hours 15 minutes

Servings: 24 pinwheels

Ingredients

- 3 large flour tortillas

Filling

- 8 oz package of cream cheese
- 1/2 cup grated parmesan cheese
- ½ cup shredded cooked chicken
- ¼ teaspoon salt
- ½ teaspoon garlic powder

Instructions

Add the pinwheel filling ingredients into a large bowl. Mix well until incorporated. The cream cheese should be softened at room temperature to be easy to work with.

Lay your tortillas on the working surface and divide the filling mixture among them. Make sure to spread it evenly.

Roll each tortilla tightly and wrap it with plastic wrap.

Let the filled tortillas chill in the fridge for at least 2 hours to make slicing easier.

When the tortillas are chilled, remove the wrap and slice them into 1-inch pieces. Serve and enjoy.

11. Vegetable pinwheels

Combining broccoli and red pepper adds tons of flavor to this pinwheel recipe. You can always switch with other veggies if you're feeling creative enough. After all, cooking is about experimenting and finding what works best for you.

Time: 2 hours 15 minutes

Servings: 24 pinwheels

Ingredients

- 3 large flour tortillas

Filling

- 8 oz package of cream cheese
- 1 cup grated cheddar cheese
- 1 cup chopped broccoli and red pepper mix
- ¼ teaspoon salt
- ½ teaspoon garlic powder
- ½ teaspoon onion powder
- 1 tablespoon chopped dill

Instructions

Add the pinwheel filling ingredients into a large bowl. Mix well until incorporated. The cream cheese should be softened at room temperature to be easy to work with.

Lay your tortillas on the working surface and divide the filling mixture among them. Make sure to spread it evenly.

Roll each tortilla tightly and wrap it with plastic wrap.

Let the filled tortillas chill in the fridge for at least 2 hours to make slicing easier.

When the tortillas are chilled, remove the wrap and slice them into 1-inch pieces. Serve and enjoy.

12. Chicken mayo pinwheels

The chicken mayo pinwheels are your way to go when you're looking for an easy appetizer to serve at a birthday party. These pinwheels are crowd pleaser, and everyone will enjoy their taste.

Time: 2 hours 15 minutes

Servings: 24 pinwheels

Ingredients

- 3 large flour tortillas
- 12 slices ham

Filling

- 4 oz of cream cheese
- ⅓ cup mayonnaise
- 1 cup shredded cooked chicken
- ½ cup grated hard cheese
- ¼ teaspoon salt
- ½ teaspoon garlic powder
- ½ teaspoon onion powder
- 1 teaspoon dried parsley

Instructions

Add the pinwheel filling ingredients into a large bowl. Mix well until incorporated. The cream cheese should be softened at room temperature to be easy to work with.

Lay your tortillas on the working surface and divide the filling mixture among them. Make sure to spread it evenly.

Roll each tortilla tightly and wrap it with plastic wrap.

Let the filled tortillas chill in the fridge for at least 2 hours to make slicing easier.

When the tortillas are chilled, remove the wrap and slice them into 1-inch pieces. Serve and enjoy.

13. Greek salad pinwheels

The combination of feta cheese, olives, and cucumber will introduce freshness to your party table. These simple yet tasty pinwheels are ideal for serving your guests.

Time: 2 hours 15 minutes

Servings: 24 pinwheels

Ingredients

- 3 large flour tortillas

Filling

- 8 oz crumbled feta cheese
- 1/2 cup greek yogurt
- ½ cup chopped olives
- ¼ teaspoon salt
- ½ teaspoon oregano
- ½ teaspoon garlic powder
- 1 tablespoon finely chopped onion
- ¾ cup finely chopped cucumber
- 1 tablespoon finely chopped parsley

Instructions

Add the pinwheel filling ingredients into a large bowl. Mix well until incorporated. The cream cheese should be softened at room temperature to be easy to work with.

Lay your tortillas on the working surface and divide the filling mixture among them. Make sure to spread it evenly.

Roll each tortilla tightly and wrap it with plastic wrap.

Let the filled tortillas chill in the fridge for at least 2 hours to make slicing easier.

When the tortillas are chilled, remove the wrap and slice them into 1-inch pieces. Serve and enjoy.

14. Deli turkey pinwheels

The trick to the perfect pinwheels is the softened cream cheese. The mixture will be lumpy and uneven if you forget to leave it to soften at room temperature. When the pinwheels chill in the freezer, the mixture will harden and allow easy slicing.

Time: 2 hours 15 minutes

Servings: 24 pinwheels

Ingredients

- 3 large flour tortillas
- ½ lb. thinly sliced deli turkey

Filling

- 8 oz package of cream cheese
- 1 tablespoon mayonnaise
- 1 cup shredded cheddar cheese
- ½ cup cooked and crumbled bacon
- ¼ teaspoon salt
- ½ teaspoon garlic powder

Instructions

Add the pinwheel filling ingredients into a large bowl. Mix well until incorporated. The cream cheese should be softened at room temperature to be easy to work with.

Lay your tortillas on the working surface and layer the deli turkey on top. Divide the filling mixture among them. Make sure to spread it evenly.

Roll each tortilla tightly and wrap it with plastic wrap.

Let the filled tortillas chill in the fridge for at least 2 hours to make slicing easier.

When the tortillas are chilled, remove the wrap and slice them into 1-inch pieces. Serve and enjoy.

15. Cranberry pinwheels

When you're looking for a unique gourmet pleasure, the combination of turkey, Havarti cheese, and cranberries will be an ideal fit. You can switch the cheese with any other neutral cheese to meet your needs.

Time: 2 hours 15 minutes

Servings: 24 pinwheels

Ingredients

- 3 large flour tortillas
- 12 oz turkey deli
- 8 oz Havarti cheese slices

Filling

- 8 oz package of cream cheese
- 1 cup shredded cheese
- 1/2 cup dried cranberries
- ¼ teaspoon salt
- 3 tablespoons chopped green onions

Instructions

Add the pinwheel filling ingredients into a large bowl. Mix well until incorporated. The cream cheese should be softened at room temperature to be easy to work with.

Lay your tortillas on the working surface and layer the turkey and cheese. Divide the filling mixture among them. Make sure to spread it evenly.

Roll each tortilla tightly and wrap it with plastic wrap.

Let the filled tortillas chill in the fridge for at least 2 hours to make slicing easier.

When the tortillas are chilled, remove the wrap and slice them into 1-inch pieces. Serve and enjoy.

16. Taco pinwheels

The taco seasoning, Colby jack cheese, and olives merge to create delicious finger food ready to be served at your parties. The recipe is enough for 24 pieces, but you can double for more.

Time: 2 hours 15 minutes

Servings: 24 pinwheels

Ingredients

- 3 large flour tortillas

Filling

- 8 oz package of cream cheese
- 1 cup shredded Colby Jack cheese
- ⅓ cup Greek yogurt
- ½ cup chopped olives
- 2 tablespoons taco seasoning
- ¼ teaspoon salt
- 2 tablespoons sliced green onions

Instructions

Add the pinwheel filling ingredients into a large bowl. Mix well until incorporated. The cream cheese should be softened at room temperature to be easy to work with.

Lay your tortillas on the working surface and divide the filling mixture among them. Make sure to spread it evenly.

Roll each tortilla tightly and wrap it with plastic wrap.

Let the filled tortillas chill in the fridge for at least 2 hours to make slicing easier.

When the tortillas are chilled, remove the wrap and slice them into 1-inch pieces. Serve and enjoy.

17. Salami pinwheels

A layer of salami covered with aromatic cream cheese is a tasty appetizer for your guests. But also, you can pack this in your kid's lunchbox. Everyone will love the classic combination of cream cheese, ham, and pickles.

Time: 2 hours 15 minutes

Servings: 24 pinwheels

Ingredients

- 3 large flour tortillas
- 12 slices salami

Filling

- 8 oz package of cream cheese
- ½ cup chopped dill pickles
- ¼ teaspoon salt

Instructions

Add the pinwheel filling ingredients into a large bowl. Mix well until incorporated. The cream cheese should be softened at room temperature to be easy to work with.

Lay your tortillas on the working surface and layer the salami slices. Divide the filling mixture among them. Make sure to spread it evenly.

Roll each tortilla tightly and wrap it with plastic wrap.

Let the filled tortillas chill in the fridge for at least 2 hours to make slicing easier.

When the tortillas are chilled, remove the wrap and slice them into 1-inch pieces. Serve and enjoy.

18. Spicy turkey pinwheels

When you like spicy pinwheels, these recipes will amaze you. You can adjust the hot sauce to your preference for the perfect flavor. Also, you can switch the turkey deli with ham or salami if you wish.

Time: 2 hours 15 minutes

Servings: 24 pinwheels

Ingredients

- 3 large flour tortillas
- 12 slices of turkey deli

Filling

- 8 oz package of cream cheese
- 1 teaspoon hot sauce, or to your preference
- 1 teaspoon smoked paprika
- ½ cup chopped roasted red peppers
- ¼ teaspoon salt

Instructions

Add the pinwheel filling ingredients into a large bowl. Mix well until incorporated. The cream cheese should be softened at room temperature to be easy to work with.

Lay your tortillas on the working surface and divide the filling mixture among them. Make sure to spread it evenly.

Roll each tortilla tightly and wrap it with plastic wrap.

Let the filled tortillas chill in the fridge for at least 2 hours to make slicing easier.

When the tortillas are chilled, remove the wrap and slice them into 1-inch pieces. Serve and enjoy.

19. Ham pinwheels

The simple yet flavorful combination is ideal for serving at a house party. Together with good drinks, it will provide an enjoyable gourmet experience for everyone.

Time: 2 hours 15 minutes

Servings: 24 pinwheels

Ingredients

- 3 large flour tortillas
- 12 slices ham

Filling

- 8 oz package of cream cheese
- 1 tablespoon mayonnaise
- ½ cup chopped olives
- ¼ teaspoon salt
- ½ teaspoon garlic powder

Instructions

Add the pinwheel filling ingredients into a large bowl. Mix well until incorporated. The cream cheese should be softened at room temperature to be easy to work with.

Lay your tortillas on the working surface and layer the ham slices. Divide the filling mixture among them. Make sure to spread it evenly.

Roll each tortilla tightly and wrap it with plastic wrap.

Let the filled tortillas chill in the fridge for at least 2 hours to make slicing easier.

When the tortillas are chilled, remove the wrap and slice them into 1-inch pieces. Serve and enjoy.

20. Cucumber pinwheels

The simple yet flavorful combination is ideal for serving as an appetizer, complementing a charcuterie board. It doesn't have meat, but you can add ham or turkey deli if you wish to.

Time: 2 hours 15 minutes

Servings: 24 pinwheels

Ingredients

- 3 large flour tortillas
- 2 medium cucumbers, thinly sliced

Filling

- 8 oz package of cream cheese
- ¼ teaspoon salt
- 1 teaspoon garlic powder

Instructions

Add the pinwheel filling ingredients into a large bowl. Mix well until incorporated. The cream cheese should be softened at room temperature to be easy to work with.

Lay your tortillas on the working surface and layer the thinly sliced cucumber. Divide the filling mixture among them. Make sure to spread it evenly.

Roll each tortilla tightly and wrap it with plastic wrap.

Let the filled tortillas chill in the fridge for at least 2 hours to make slicing easier.

When the tortillas are chilled, remove the wrap and slice them into 1-inch pieces. Serve and enjoy.

21. Bacon mayo pinwheels

The crumbled bacon and mayonnaise will add extra flavor to this pinwheel recipe. You are free to use any hard cheese that suits your preference here.

Time: 2 hours 15 minutes

Servings: 24 pinwheels

Ingredients

- 3 large flour tortillas

Filling

- 8 oz package of cream cheese
- 1/2 cup shredded hard cheese
- 2 tablespoons mayonnaise
- ½ cup cooked and crumbled bacon
- ¼ teaspoon salt
- 1 teaspoon onion powder
- ½ teaspoon smoked paprika

Instructions

Add the pinwheel filling ingredients into a large bowl. Mix well until incorporated. The cream cheese should be softened at room temperature to be easy to work with.

Lay your tortillas on the working surface and divide the filling mixture among them. Make sure to spread it evenly.

Roll each tortilla tightly and wrap it with plastic wrap.

Let the filled tortillas chill in the fridge for at least 2 hours to make slicing easier.

When the tortillas are chilled, remove the wrap and slice them into 1-inch pieces. Serve and enjoy.

22. Four cheeses pinwheels

The flavorful filling that contains four kinds of cheese will create a decadent appetizer for fine dining. If you want to feel that gooey cheesy texture, feel free to heat them in the oven for a couple of minutes until the cheese melts.

Time: 2 hours 15 minutes

Servings: 24 pinwheels

Ingredients

- 3 large flour tortillas

Filling

- 8 oz package of cream cheese
- 1/2 cup shredded hard cheese
- ¼ cup grated parmesan
- ¼ cup crumbled blue cheese
- ¼ cup shredded mozzarella

Instructions

Add the pinwheel filling ingredients into a large bowl. Mix well until incorporated. The cream cheese should be softened at room temperature to be easy to work with.

Lay your tortillas on the working surface and divide the filling mixture among them. Make sure to spread it evenly.

Roll each tortilla tightly and wrap it with plastic wrap.

Let the filled tortillas chill in the fridge for at least 2 hours to make slicing easier.

When the tortillas are chilled, remove the wrap and slice them into 1-inch pieces. Serve and enjoy.

23. Cauliflower pinwheels

Combining broccoli and cauliflower will add tons of flavor to this pinwheels recipe. You can add extra veggies such as red pepper and carrot to achieve a vibrantly colorful look.

Time: 2 hours 15 minutes

Servings: 24 pinwheels

Ingredients

- 3 large flour tortillas

Filling

- 8 oz package of cream cheese
- 1 cup shredded cheese
- ½ cup finely chopped broccoli
- ½ cup finely chopped cauliflower
- ½ red pepper finely chopped
- 1 tablespoon ranch dressing
- ¼ teaspoon salt

Instructions

Add the pinwheel filling ingredients into a large bowl. Mix well until incorporated. The cream cheese should be softened at room temperature to be easy to work with.

Lay your tortillas on the working surface and divide the filling mixture among them. Make sure to spread it evenly.

Roll each tortilla tightly and wrap it with plastic wrap.

Let the filled tortillas chill in the fridge for at least 2 hours to make slicing easier.

When the tortillas are chilled, remove the wrap and slice them into 1-inch pieces. Serve and enjoy.

24. Hummus pinwheels

The hummus pinwheels are the best choice if you need a vegan option to serve at your party. Even if you don't have vegan friends, remember that everyone will love the aromatic hummus pinwheels.

Time: 2 hours 15 minutes

Servings: 24 pinwheels

Ingredients

- 3 large flour tortillas

Filling

- ¾ cup hummus
- ¼ cup baby spinach, chopped
- ½ cucumber, finely chopped
- ½ cup sun-dried tomatoes finely chopped

Instructions

Add the pinwheel filling ingredients into a large bowl. Mix well until incorporated. The cream cheese should be softened at room temperature to be easy to work with.

Lay your tortillas on the working surface and divide the filling mixture among them. Make sure to spread it evenly.

Roll each tortilla tightly. Slice them into 1-inch pieces. Serve and enjoy.

25. Spicy hummus pinwheels

The spicy version of the humus pinwheels is a tasty appetizer to serve at your party. You can adjust the hot sauce depending on how strong you want the pinwheels to be.

Time: 2 hours 15 minutes

Servings: 24 pinwheels

Ingredients

- 3 large flour tortillas

Filling

- ¾ cup hummus
- 1 teaspoon hot sauce
- ½ teaspoon pepper flakes
- 1 roasted red pepper, finely chopped

Instructions

Add the pinwheel filling ingredients into a large bowl. Mix well until incorporated. The cream cheese should be softened at room temperature to be easy to work with.

Lay your tortillas on the working surface and divide the filling mixture among them. Make sure to spread it evenly.

Roll each tortilla tightly and wrap it with plastic wrap.

Let the filled tortillas chill in the fridge for at least 2 hours to make slicing easier.

When the tortillas are chilled, remove the wrap and slice them into 1-inch pieces. Serve and enjoy.

26. Pesto pinwheels

The aromatic flavor of pesto will enhance this simple pinwheels recipe. The combination of parmesan, sun-dried tomatoes, and pesto will bring the Italian flavors to your table.

Time: 2 hours 15 minutes

Servings: 24 pinwheels

Ingredients

- 3 large flour tortillas

Filling

- 8 oz package of cream cheese
- 1/2 cup grated parmesan cheese
- 1/2 cup pesto
- ¼ cup chopped sundried tomatoes

Instructions

Add the pinwheel filling ingredients into a large bowl. Mix well until incorporated. The cream cheese should be softened at room temperature to be easy to work with.

Lay your tortillas on the working surface and divide the filling mixture among them. Make sure to spread it evenly.

Roll each tortilla tightly and wrap it with plastic wrap.

Let the filled tortillas chill in the fridge for at least 2 hours to make slicing easier.

When the tortillas are chilled, remove the wrap and slice them into 1-inch pieces. Serve and enjoy.

27. Smoked salmon pinwheels

Try the smoked salmon pinwheels when you wish to serve an elegant appetizer for a fine dining experience at home. The simple flavor combination will amaze even the ones with the most refined taste.

Time: 2 hours 15 minutes

Servings: 24 pinwheels

Ingredients

- 3 large flour tortillas
- 12 slices of smoked salmon

Filling

- 8 oz package of cream cheese
- ½ cup chopped dill
- ¼ teaspoon salt

Instructions

Add the pinwheel filling ingredients into a large bowl. Mix well until incorporated. The cream cheese should be softened at room temperature to be easy to work with.

Lay your tortillas on the working surface and divide the filling mixture among them. Make sure to spread it evenly.

Roll each tortilla tightly and wrap it with plastic wrap.

Let the filled tortillas chill in the fridge for at least 2 hours to make slicing easier.

When the tortillas are chilled, remove the wrap and slice them into 1-inch pieces. Serve and enjoy.

28. Chicken pesto pinwheels

The chicken and pesto combination creates a symphony of flavors, ready to be served at your gathering. But also, you can prepare a double batch of these for a potluck.

Time: 2 hours 15 minutes

Servings: 24 pinwheels

Ingredients

- 3 large flour tortillas

Filling

- 8 oz package of cream cheese
- 1 cup shredded and cooked chicken
- ½ cup sundried tomatoes
- ½ cup pesto
- ¼ teaspoon salt

Instructions

Add the pinwheel filling ingredients into a large bowl. Mix well until incorporated. The cream cheese should be softened at room temperature to be easy to work with.

Lay your tortillas on the working surface and divide the filling mixture among them. Make sure to spread it evenly.

Roll each tortilla tightly and wrap it with plastic wrap.

Let the filled tortillas chill in the fridge for at least 2 hours to make slicing easier.

When the tortillas are chilled, remove the wrap and slice them into 1-inch pieces. Serve and enjoy.

29. Caesar pinwheels

If you like the standard caesar salad, you will love these pinwheels inspired by the recipe. With lettuce, dressing, chicken, and parmesan, they are a gourmet pleasure for your fine dining experience.

Time: 2 hours 15 minutes

Servings: 24 pinwheels

Ingredients

- 3 large flour tortillas
- 6 leaves lettuce

Filling

- 8 oz package of cream cheese
- 2 tablespoons caesar salad dressing
- 1 cup shredded cooked chicken
- ½ cup grated parmesan

Instructions

Add the pinwheel filling ingredients into a large bowl. Mix well until incorporated. The cream cheese should be softened at room temperature to be easy to work with.

Lay your tortillas on the working surface and divide the filling mixture among them. Make sure to spread it evenly.

Roll each tortilla tightly and wrap it with plastic wrap.

Let the filled tortillas chill in the fridge for at least 2 hours to make slicing easier.

When the tortillas are chilled, remove the wrap and slice them into 1-inch pieces. Serve and enjoy.

30. Green pinwheels

The green filling is a tasty combination of cooked spinach, cheese, and cream cheese. It is a vegetarian option to serve as an addition to the main dish or delicious finger food with white wine.

Time: 2 hours 15 minutes

Servings: 24 pinwheels

Ingredients

- 3 large flour tortillas

Filling

- 8 oz package of cream cheese
- 1 cup shredded jack Colby cheese
- 4 cups spinach, cooked
- ¼ teaspoon salt
- ½ teaspoon garlic powder

Instructions

Add the pinwheel filling ingredients into a large bowl. Mix well until incorporated. The cream cheese should be softened at room temperature to be easy to work with.

Lay your tortillas on the working surface and divide the filling mixture among them. Make sure to spread it evenly.

Roll each tortilla tightly and wrap it with plastic wrap.

Let the filled tortillas chill in the fridge for at least 2 hours to make slicing easier.

When the tortillas are chilled, remove the wrap and slice them into 1-inch pieces. Serve and enjoy.

Conclusion

With these fantastic pinwheel recipes, you can prepare delicious appetizers to feed a crowd. But you can also experiment with the different options and consume a healthy lunch prepared by yourself. The pinwheels are a portable lunch idea for the whole family.

With lots of flavors to choose from, you can find the right fit for your mood. Sometimes you might crave spicy buffalo chicken flavor. Or you might want salmon pinwheels to complement a fine white wine glass. Or you can prepare cucumber pinwheels to appeal to anyone's taste.

You learned that the secret to the best texture is using softened cream cheese. But also, you knew that chilling the pinwheels in the fridge for at least two hours will help you cut perfect round slices. This recipe book shares the best flavor combinations and teaches you how to prepare the best appetizers. Now you're ready to amaze a crowd and serve delicious finger foods.

If you like this recipe book, don't forget to check our extensive collection. You will find something that matches your taste!

Author's Afterthoughts

thank you

Now's the moment of truth… What did you think about my cookbook? Did you like the recipes in it? While I certainly hope so, I would also like to know what you'd like to see more of! This might come as a surprise to you, but your ideas will surely inspire my upcoming cookbooks since the only reason I write is so that you can try out my dishes! Without you, I certainly wouldn't be here–writing and all.

Perhaps you'd like a cookbook to help you with weight loss or to help you stick to the Keto diet while eating delicious meals…Or maybe you'd just like to see a whole cookbook on brunch recipes or overnight breakfasts… You're the boss!

The only reason I can write cookbooks and try new recipes for a living is because of you, so now is my time to show some gratitude by creating cookbooks that will actually help you get through your weekly meals or special occasions! Just let us know what you'd like to see more of, and you can bet we'll get your ideas to the drawing board.

Thanks,

Tristan

About the Author

Tristan grew up watching his dad and grandma spend hours in the kitchen before a family gathering. They would prepare some of granny's secret family recipes together and then serve them once everyone arrived. Tristan only chopped carrots and onions for them, occasionally stirring the pots too, but he didn't realize how important his job was until he grew up and found himself needing a hand in the kitchen.

Especially when living on your own, doing all the chopping and cooking yourself can be very tiring. While he wished his cat could lend him a paw, hairballs weren't exactly part of his weekly night menu. For some time, Tristan lived off take-out food because it was convenient. After a long day of work, who wants to spend another hour preparing dinner and then washing the dishes? It wasn't until a buddy of his, who also happened to live on his own, introduced him into the world of meal preps and easy, simple dinners that Tristan's life changed.

He started cooking for himself. Nothing fancy, just quick but healthy meals that didn't make him dread coming home to make dinner. The cleanup was easy, too, since it was mostly one-pot meals. Eventually, he started to freeze his meals for the entire month, only reheating them as needed. His colleagues started to pick up on this, and they were soon asking Tristan to make their weekly lunch and dinners too!

Though he never envisioned himself as a full-time cook, Tristan now runs his own meal prep company in California, preparing over 1,000 meals per week for busy people who want healthy homemade meals. Occasionally, his dad goes to help out in the kitchen, now only letting him chop carrots and onions, occasionally stirring the pots too, and Tristan can't believe how lucky he is to have a helping hand like his.

❯◉◉◉◉◉◉◉◉◉◉◉◉◉◉◉◉◉◉◉◉◉❮

Printed in Great Britain
by Amazon